KEEP OR INVEST THE MONEY? IT IS NO LONGER A DILEMMA!!!

How to be more competitive without dying while trying?

ALEXANDER FERNANDEZ, MBA

Copyright © 2020 Víctor Alexander Fernández Paravecino

Todos los derechos reservados.

ISBN: 979-8-6506-0239-2

DEDICATION

For everybody who always seek and never sleep.

CONTENTS

	Agradecimientos	i
1	Página del título	1
2	Introducción	9
3	Prólogo	11
4	Conceptos básicos	12
5	Fundamentos teóricos	15
6	Conclusiones	32
7	Referencias	36
8	Acerca del autor	40

ACKNOWLEDGEMENT

Thanks to my family and friends that support me everyday.
Thanks God for being always there.

INTRODUCTION

The world moves in a dynamic environment in which an individual finds it difficult to make decisions about the lack of information and understanding of the events around them, there is much uncertainty in the environment surrounding companies, this uncertainty affects the manage of the money because this is the end result of the decisions, as we know there are companies that go bankrupt for lack of money, a company can have a good financial condition but not necessarily a healthy cash, it would be then a right decision to keep money or simply to have what its needed, but what is really needed? for that reason this book intends to show if making and keeping money is convenient unlike maintain a minimum cash after investments just to meet the needs of the

KEEP OR INVEST THE MONEY? IT IS NO LONGER A DILEMMA!!!

company considering the variants that affects liquidity, the cost of capital, etc. For this, the positions of different authors will be discussed and we will conclude with the answer to this dilemma.

KEEP OR INVEST THE MONEY? IT IS NO LONGER A DILEMMA!!!

FOREWORD

As advisors we are always asked by management or the owners of the companies if we should keep the cash or if we should invest it, many financial managers recommend not having a lot of money because it means that the cash is working and is generating a return for the company but in saying this, are they considering the uncertainty of the environment?.

At a time before Christ, Heraclitus said that the only constant is change. If this was said thousands of years ago, it is much more reason to take more account of uncertainty and always keep it in mind in our business strategies.

KEEP OR INVEST THE MONEY? IT IS NO LONGER A DILEMMA!!!

BASIC CONCEPTS

We will first define the types of uncertainty, for Milliken (as cited in Ashill & Jobber, 2014) he distinguished three types of uncertainty, from: (a) state, (b) effect, and (c) response and mentioned:

> State uncertainty describes a situation where managers do not feel confident that they understand what the major events or trends in an environment are, or feel unable to accurately assign probabilities to the likelihood that those particular events or changes will occur… Effect uncertainty reflects a lack of understanding of how the future state of the environment may affect the organization, that is, a lack of understanding of cause–effect relationships. Response

uncertainty is experienced when managers do not know the range of strategic responses open to them and/or are unable to evaluate their relative utility. (p.269)

Profit and cash flow generally do not seem go together, many managers and owners wonder why if I have profits I do not have money, in certain cases there are companies where there is an increase in profits but they have a negative cash flow, that is because in growing businesses start investing to sell more and begin to be financed because the benefits are insufficient for these porpouses, besides the sellings are not be completly collected. There is also the opposite where the results are lower than the cash flow, which are more recurring in companies in mature stages where there is disposal of investments.

Regarding the cost of keeping money, it refers to the opportunity cost that is defined as the maximum sacrifice that one makes, for example a worker is sacrificing the time to spend with his family or friends for being in a company performing his functions. In this case if we keep cash on hand, we are sacrificing an interest rate that would be charged for having lent that money or have invested in a project or title negotiable, in other words the

KEEP OR INVEST THE MONEY? IT IS NO LONGER A DILEMMA!!!

money is not working.

THEORETICAL FOUNDATIONS

In general companies are advised to manage cash, recommending that they keep the lowest level of money without affecting the operation of the company, in other words, they collect early and pay late, and if there are cash surpluses, companies invest in some bank product or negotiable instrument in short term or paid dividends to the owners or shareholders.

Just as data when the 2008 recession occurred due to the housing bubble, Ford had a balance of cash and cash equivalents of $ 24.9 billion, Microsoft $ 21 billion and General Electric $ 60 billion, these firms had large amounts of cash and cash equivalents due to their management (Ross, Westerfield & Jaffe, 2012).

KEEP OR INVEST THE MONEY? IT IS NO LONGER A DILEMMA!!!

According to Keynes (as cited in Ross, Westerfield & Jaffe, 2012) in his classic work *The General Theory of Employment, Interest and Money*, there are three reasons for maintaining liquidity: the speculative reason, precautionary reason and the reason for the transaction. The speculative reason is the need for cash to take advantage of bargains, attractive interest rates, or favorable exchange rate fluctuations. The precautionary reason is the need to have a security provision that acts as a financial reserve. The reason for the transaction is the need to have cash for recurring expenses such as operating expenses to pay salaries and payrolls, commercial debts, taxes and dividends.

The types of uncertainty, mentioned by Milliken previously ((a) state, (b) effect, and (c) response), have their effects on the decision making of the cash management of the companies and as a consequence they need instruments to make decisions within of an uncertain environment, however in these times there is so much uncertainty, that the decision maker could not assign exact probabilities. As a consequence, the tools used may not be applied correctly. In the case of the Capital Asset Pricing Model [CAPM] in emerging economies, it is used to make important decisions in order to know the value of a company as well as the viability of a project taking into account how much is the minimum that the shareholder should ask for his investment or if the company is generating added value as well as other uses, however this model is based on a priori or expected conditions, despite the fact that it has just retrospective or past data. The betas used in the CAPM model show the volatility of a stock in the past, however conditions could change. Future volatility of stocks, which is what investors are really interested in, could differ radically from their past volatility (Besley & Brigham, 2013).

The most outstanding uncertainty characteristics of emerging countries are:

- the volatility of the currency,
- country risk,
- unreliable market measures due to illiquidity,
- accounting differences and lack of information,
- lack of corporate governance, and

- discontinuous risk that apart from volatility there are minimal risks but with catastrophic effects such as expropriation or terrorism.

There are other problems of the analyst when it comes to valuing companies in these markets, such as:

- exchange rate disparity,
- not count or consider double or triple country risk,
- risk parameters for both equity and debt,
- incorporation of effects not considering where operations are carried out,
- ignore missing information,
- changes in corporate governance, and
- do not consider post valuation discounts (Damodaran, 2009).

It should be noted that in emerging markets, the historical returns of their own stock markets cannot be used to calculate the market risk premium due to their high volatility (Bravo, 2008). All this framework of uncertainty and the lack of reliability in the CAPM model due to the fact that it uses a historical beta and the volatility in emerging countries forces the use of more tools such as sensitivity analysis or others as approximations

According to the studies of Duchin (2015) mentioned:

CASH HOLDINGS OF U.S. companies are enormous and growing over time. As of fiscal year 2006, nonfinancial and nonutility firms in the Compustat universe reported aggregate cash holdings of over 1.7 trillion dollars, representing 9.2% of the total market value of these firms' equity. The growth in cash holdings is equally impressive… listed U.S. industrial firms' average ratio of cash to assets increased from 10.5% in 1980 to 23.2% in 2006… While the dramatic increase in cash holdings is receiving growing attention, another noteworthy pattern is not widely recognized: The average cash holdings of stand-alone firms are almost double the cash holdings of diversified firms. From 1990 to 2006, diversified firms held on average 11.9% of their assets in cash, whereas stand-alone firms held more than 20.9% of their assets. (p. 955)

According to these statistics, a large increase in companies that maintain cash has been seen, however, among these companies are stand-alone firms and others diversified, as we can see in Figure 1 the cash that stand-alone companies maintain is double that the diversified firms since they use the cash for differents projects reducing nad distributing the risk of having just one project.

Duchin (2015) suggested in their conclusions that diversified companies reduce their cash flow to optimal levels positively affecting the value of these companies because they save on the costs of keeping cash and induce their managers to manage themselves optimally.

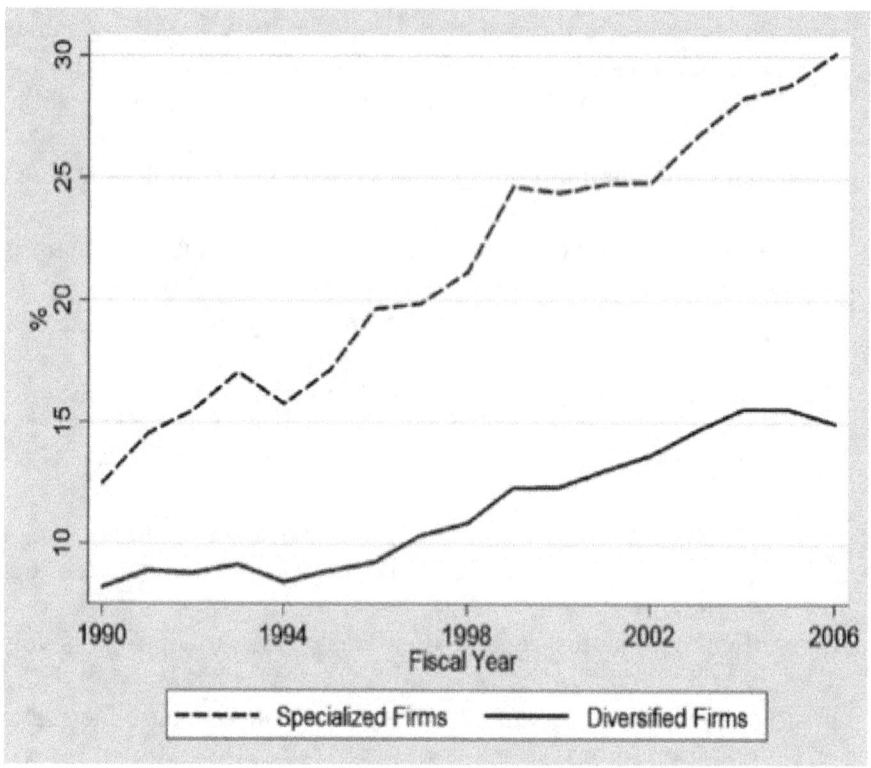

Figure 1. Annual average of cash balances (%) of specialized and diversified companies

<u>Note.</u> Of The Journal of Finance Vol. LXV, N° 3, June 2010

According to Keynes's theory (as quoted in Duchin, 2015), companies hold cash to protect themselves from adverse cash flow impacts that could force them to abandon good investment opportunities due to the cost of external financing. According to Herrera (s.f.) excess cash balances should be avoided since they are generally not adequately profitable and it hardly reaches the cost of capital of the company. Complementing it, Herrera (2014) mentioned that the cost of keeping idle balances in account is detrimental to the company as at least the company must expect profitability higher than its weighted average cost of capital and that the treasurer should look for innovative solutions from its financial providers that allow to manage your liquidity surpluses.

Edwards (2014) mentioned to us how important it is to have cash on hand and how fast a company can go bankrupt, he concluded:

> It has been said that "revenue is vanity, cash flow is sanity." Making sure your company has enough cash to keep evolving, growing, and moving forward is very important… Of course, if your company is highly profitable and spitting cash (like Apple), then this whole issue is not as important. But companies can go from profits to losses very quickly because of a bad economy or a product-cycle transition or some other bad fortune. When that happens, burn rate can become important. So having a sense of cash movements is always a good idea. (p. 9)

According to the studies by Chittenden and Derregia (2015), they concluded that in the assessment of uncertainty, companies commonly use scenario analysis, either alone or together with sensitivity analysis, with a minority of companies using decision trees. It was also mentioned that companies identify: (a) uncertainty in demand, (b) lack of internal financing, and (c) uncertainty in interest rates as importants in delaying investment decisions. However, the number of companies using these techniques to assess uncertainty exceeds the number of companies using simple capital budgeting techniques. It was also mentioned that there is an observed decrease in capital expenditures in companies in times of economic uncertainty.

In his study, Bloom (2014) concluded that uncertainty tends to rise sharply in times of recession at macro and micro levels, amplifying the recession and reducing growth, it also varies strongly across countries, with developing countries having a third more uncertainty than developed countries. Regions like Africa and South America tend to have the most volatile gross domestic product, stock market and exchange rates. Additionally, too much uncertainty reduces the decisions of companies to hire and invest, as well as consumers to spend.

According to Hsu, Huang and Lai (2015) implied that an independent board of directors or a finance committee would allow managers to maintain excess cash to avoid problems of lack of investment due to lack of cash. Their studies also supported the argument that once growth opportunities are anticipated, an independent board or committee of funders would choose to maintain excess cash to avoid high external financing.

In the Kim & Betis (2014) research, it was mentioned that companies face external uncertainty in macroeconomic conditions, demand, regulation, legislation, new competitors, energy costs, etc. For example, when a firm faces an uncertainty decision such as choosing between two new technological production alternatives, here it can use cash as a buffer to delay the decision until the uncertainty is adequately resolved. It was also added that according to nature there are companies that constantly face high levels of uncertainty, in these terms the most representative companies would be those related to rapid innovation such as pharmaceuticals, technology, etc. Furthermore, it was mentioned that research and development companies can have high returns for maintaining cash and this effect is amplified with increasing uncertainty. Idle cash balances encourage innovation by facilitating risky projects. The results of these studies suggested that keeping cash in large companies become more valuable as a competitive strategy resource.

There are other studies such as those carried out by Foerster (2014) where it also concluded that high uncertainty during a recovery period has led to a decreased recovery. Uncertainty has an asymmetric effect, which suggests that the decrease in uncertainty does not necessarily compensate for the effects when the uncertainty increased. As can be seen in Figure 2 the volatility index rises in recessions and tends to decrease during the recovery, however it experiences short fluctuations.

Probabilities are the language of uncertainty according to Salinas (2008):

La incertidumbre es una consecuencia del conocimiento

incompleto del mundo que nos rodea. Si bien en algunos casos la incertidumbre puede ser eliminada parcial o totalmente antes de tomar una decisión, en la mayoría de los casos importantes la información completa simplemente no existe o es muy costosa en términos de tiempo y dinero. A menudo la gente considera que trata adecuadamente a la incertidumbre usando el lenguaje común....Para describir las incertidumbres usan frases como "es muy probable que ocurra", "hay una buena posibilidad", "ocurrirá casi con seguridad", "es posible que ocurra"... la descripción verbal de la incertidumbre tiende a ser ambigua o mal definida, por lo que es necesario tener afirmaciones probabilísticas numéricas para describir la incertidumbre en forma clara y sin ambigüedades. (pp. 75-76)

Translation:

Uncertainty is a consequence of incomplete knowledge of the world around us. While in some cases the uncertainty may be partially or totally removed before a decision is made, in most cases the complete information simply does not exist or is very costly in terms of time and money.

People often find themselves dealing adequately with uncertainty using common language .... To describe uncertainties they use phrases like "it is very likely to happen", "there is a good chance", "it will almost certainly occur", "it is possible that it happens "... the verbal description of the uncertainty tends to be ambiguous or poorly defined, so it is necessary to have numerical probabilistic statements to describe the uncertainty clearly and unambiguously. (pp. 75-76)

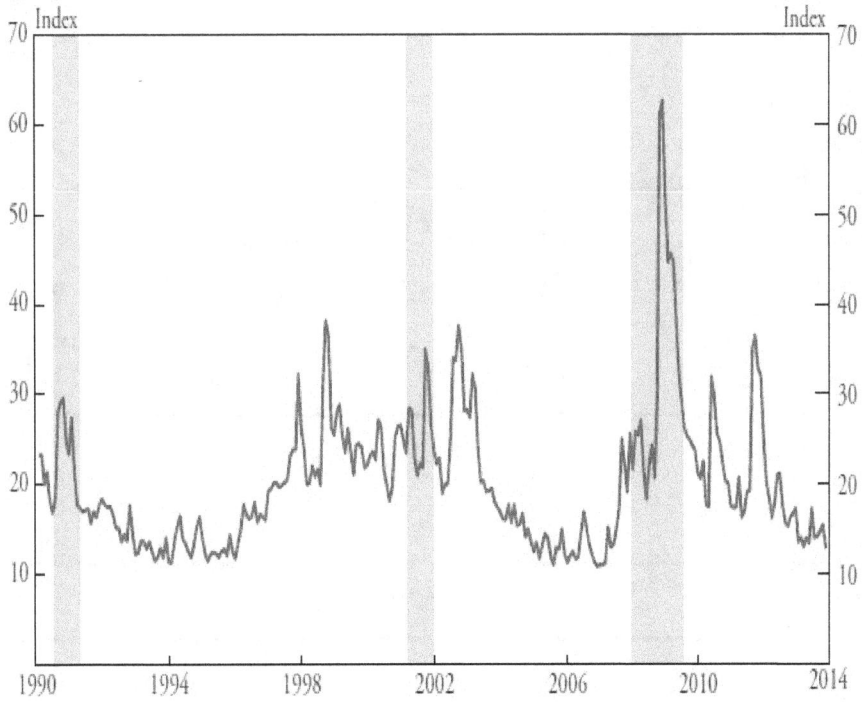

Figure 2. Gray bars represent recessions.

Note. Of Chicago Board Options Exchange

According to Salinas (2008), there are no correct probabilities since they represent the decision maker's state of knowledge about a particular event, that is, the probabilities represent the criteria and experience of a person and are not a property of the event studied. He also proposed the decision maker's reactions in a decision-making process using intuition (see Figure 3) and in a normative decision-making process of decision analysis (Figure 4).

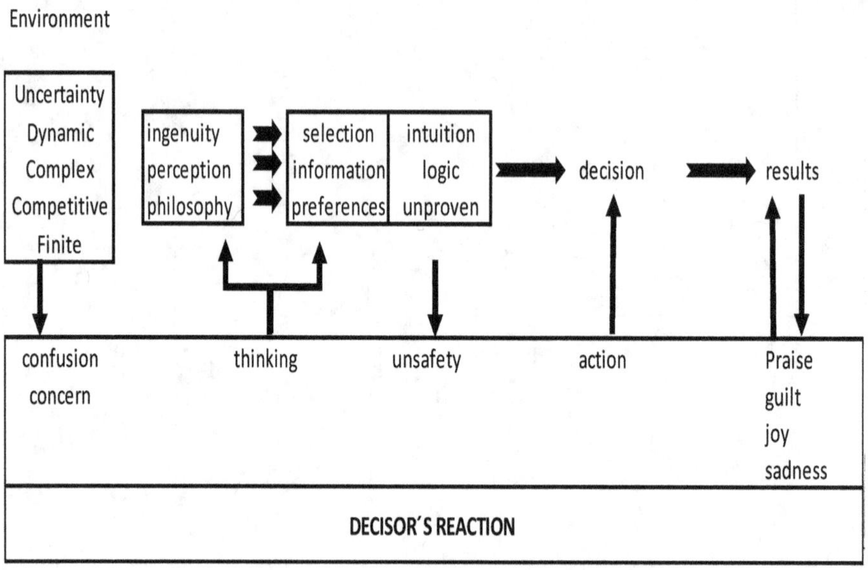

Figure 3. The decision-making process if intuition is used

Note. Of "Análisis de Decisiones estratégicas en entornos inciertos, cambiantes y complejos," by José Salinas, 2008.

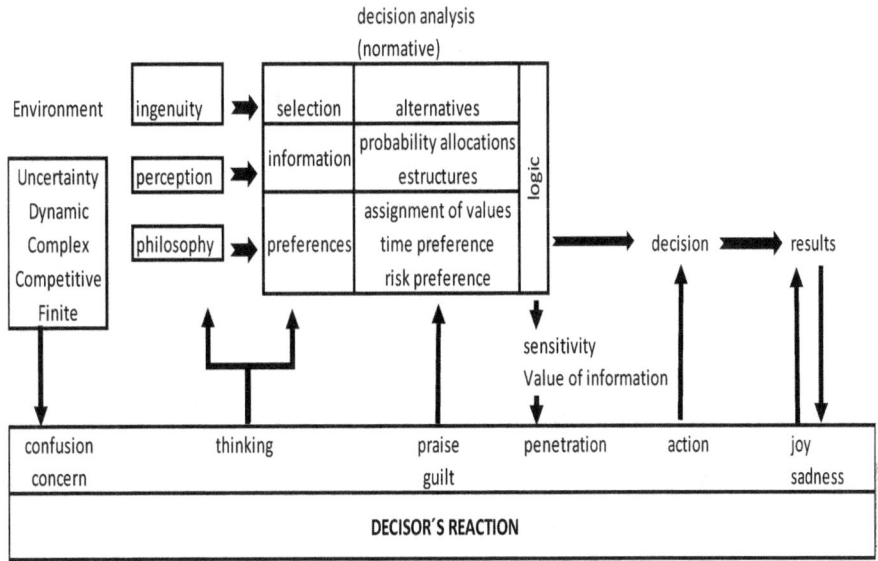

Figure 4. The normative decision-making process of decision analysis

Note. Of "Análisis de Decisiones estratégicas en entornos inciertos, cambiantes y complejos," by José Salinas, 2008.

As it is seen in the figures above, the uncertainty environment always has the same characteristics in both processes, however, in the part of the analysis of this environment in figure 3, there is no methodical analysis of the events, this is where the decision-maker is guided by his intuition, the opposite happens in figure 4 where there is a more structured, complex and verifiable analysis.

CONCLUSIONS

Uncertainty directly affects cash management and decision-making in a negative way, making companies retain more cash during periods of uncertainty because it is strategically more important for the company to survive in negative environments and take advantage of attractive investment opportunities, additionally encourages innovation and gives you strategic competition against others. It can also be added that cash management must be balanced considering probabilistic tools that may include the uncertainty of the present and the future, the treasurer being able to manage their liquidity surpluses in short-term investments as long as they can be demanded at the times that the firm need them and have a healthy distribution of dividends to the shareholders in order to maintain a healthy levels of cash with the aim of making your company more valuable. This is crucially important in developing countries which are the most affected countries in times of recession.

Uncertainty also has its negative effects on the development of the countries' economies, due to the fact that the allocation and use of resources is delayed, this uncertainty being more acute in emerging countries and without being able to have an exact measurement tool in decision-making due to the high volatility of these markets, however these measurement instruments can not be ruled out as they serve as a baseline for more complex evaluations but should only be considered as approximations. It is necessary to take into consideration the companies that are not diversified since they are the ones that have the most cash and therefore are more likely to overcome any crisis as opposed to diversified ones. Banks generally want to keep their client companies' funds at reasonable levels and not in excess since they are considered a risk because they can start investing in risky projects and lead to possible bankruptcies.

KEEP OR INVEST THE MONEY? IT IS NO LONGER A DILEMMA!!!

Having cash on hand is a way to safeguard the business, it has been seen firms to say that they have generated a lot of cash but when these firms see their financial statements these wonder where those are and the answer is in merchandise or other investment or in the distribution of dividends, Now we see that these companies cannot rotate their merchandise due to the current pandemic and need cash or restructure their debts to overcome these periods, in the same way having cash serves to take advantage of the crisis such as the purchase of other bankrupt businesses or shares that are with low prices, these purchases have an implicit form of income that will be made when it is sold as soon as prices are better or put these investments in value for sale.

Now these days there are many companies that have gone bankrupt due to the lack of money because of the pandemic, we must learn the lesson of money, having money under the mattress will save you. You can put up with negative financial results, but never lack of cash. Companies that have saved and kept money can take advantage of the uncertainty situation, as mentioned before by buying stocks that are low in price or companies that have gone bankrupt for very low values.

The survival of owners and shareholders is found in maintaining and creating cash, simply investing or spending of it would increase their risk of survival and competitive advantage. But of course, the more risk, the more profitability according to the rule, but do not risk the life of your company in new projects or investments, share that risk with other partners or shareholders despite the cost of it.

REFERENCES

Ashill, N. (2014). The effects of the external environment on marketing decision-maker uncertainty. *Journal of Marketing Management, 30*(3-4), 268-294. doi: 10.1080/0267257X.2013.811281

Besley, S. & Brigham E. (2007). *Fundamentos de administración financiera (14a. Ed.)*. México, DF, México: CENGAGE Learning.

Betis, R. & Kim, Ch. (2014). Cash is surprisingly valuable as a strategic asset. *Strategic management journal. 35*, 2053-2063. doi: 10.1002/smj.2205

Bloom, N. (2014). Fluctuations in Uncertainty. *Journal of economic perspectives. 28*(2), 153-176.

Bravo, S. (2008). *Teoría financiera y costo de capital.* Lima, Perú: Universidad ESAN.

Chittenden, F. & Derregia, M. (2013). Uncertainty, irreversibility and the use of rules of thumb in capital budgeting. *The British Accounting Review. 47*(2015), 225-236. doi:10.1016/j.bar.2013.12.003

Damodaran, A. (2009). *Volatility rules: Valuing Emerging Markets Companies.* Stern School of Business.

Duchin, R. (2010). Cash holdings and corporate diversification. *The Journal of Finance. 65*(3), 955-993.

Edward, J. (2014). Managing the cash flow gap. *The journal corporate accounting & finance, 26*(1), 3-10. doi: 10.1002/jcaf.21997

Foerster, A. (2014). The Asymmetric Effects of Uncertainty. *Federal Reserve Bank Of Kansas City Economic Review, 99*(3), 5-26.

Herrera, G. (2015). El nuevo rol del tesorero corporativo. *Revista Strategia, 8*(34), 57-60.

Herrera, G. (s.f.). Gestionando la liquidez de forma eficiente. Revista Strategia, 52-55.

Hsu, W., Huang, Y. & Lai G. (2015). Corporate governance and cash holdings: Evidence from the U.S. property – liability insurance industry. *The journal of risk and insurance. 82*(3), 715-748. doi:10.1111/jori.12049

Keynes, J. (1936). The general theory of employment, interest and money. Hartcourt Brace, London.

Milliken, F. J. (1987). Three types of uncertainty about the environment: State, effect and response uncertainty. *Academy of Management Review, 12*, 133–143. doi: 10.5465/AMR.1987.4306502

Ross, S., Westerfield, R. & Jaffe, J. (2012). Finanzas Corporativas. (9na Ed.) México: Mc Graw Hill.

Salinas, J. (2008). *Análisis de decisiones estratégicas en entornos inciertos, cambiantes y complejos (1a. Ed.)*. Buenos Aires, Argentina: CENGAGE Learning.

ABOUT THE AUTHOR

Alexander Fernández, MBA

Alex Fernández (1977) was born and grew up in Lima - Perú and lived in England for two years, He studied accountancy and MBA in Maastricht in Netherlands and Centrum Católica in Perú and has a Master in Corporate Finance in EADA from Barcelona along with CENTRUM Católica. He has authored many essays and has worked as a financial controller and Chief Financial Officer in many international and local companies. Expert in implementation projects of strategic areas with focus on business development, tax planning, financial direction and strategic, KPIs developments and all kind of solutions to the companies. Team management in different countries. Reports to International Directors and managers. Certified Public Accountant and Financial Adviser. For many years he has taught in different Universities. As hobbies, he likes to investigate different topics, to read and write, to play basketball and to meditate.

www.ingramcontent.com/pod-product-compliance
Lightning Source LLC
Chambersburg PA
CBHW081100240526
45465CB00025B/2777